One-to-one tuition

Judith Ireson

One-to-one tuition
An ideal context for learning?

Judith Ireson

Professor of Psychology in Education

Based on an Inaugural Professorial Lecture delivered at the Institute of
Education, University of London, on 16 June 2011

Institute of Education, University of London
Professorial Lecture Series

First published in 2011 by the Institute of Education, University of London,
20 Bedford Way, London WC1H 0AL
www.ioe.ac.uk/publications

British Library Cataloguing in Publication Data:
A catalogue record for this publication is available from the British Library

ISBN 978 0 85473 915 8

Typeset by Quadrant Infotech (India) Pvt Ltd
Printed by ImageData Group

Biography

Judith Ireson, PhD, AFBPsS, FRSA is Professor of Psychology in Education at the Institute of Education, University of London. After taking degrees in psychology and social anthropology she started her career as a volunteer science teacher with VSO in East Africa. Since moving into Higher Education, her research and teaching has focused on psychology in education, and she developed her thinking while working in the UK and internationally. Her work is underpinned by a longstanding interest, gained while undertaking cross-cultural research for her doctoral thesis, into relationships between social contexts and individual learning and development. She has researched and published widely on a range of topics including private tutoring, individual pedagogy, relations between pedagogical beliefs, activity and interactions, and ability grouping in education. She has directed numerous research projects funded by the Economic and Social Research Council, government departments and charitable organisations. Her recent work is concerned with the nature and extent of private tutoring, factors that influence participation in this educational activity and the quality and effectiveness of tutoring. Publications include articles in peer-reviewed academic journals and writing for wider audiences in book chapters, research briefing reports for school managers and teachers, and professional development materials. Books include *Learners, Learning and Educational Activity* (Routledge, 2008), *Ability Grouping in Education* (Paul Chapman Publishing, 2001, co-author) and *Effective Pupil Grouping in the Primary School* (Fulton, 2002, co-author).

One-to-one tuition: An ideal context for learning?

Introduction

Private tutoring is a well-established part of education for many young people in school, yet it has only recently caught the attention of researchers and policy-makers in England. During the late 1980s, achievement in US schools was lower than that in many other countries, including Japan and Germany, and much research was commissioned to discover what it was that made a difference. This research uncovered the widespread use of after-school tutoring in Japan and, as further research was undertaken, it gradually emerged that private tutoring existed in many countries. In 1999, a review commissioned by the United Nations Educational, Scientific and Cultural Organization (UNESCO) highlighted very high levels of private supplementary tutoring in some South East Asian countries (Bray, 1999). Since then, numerous reports on private tutoring have appeared around the world, and interest has grown in Europe (Bray, forthcoming 2011). The fact that the 2006 Programme for International Student Assessment (PISA) survey included questions on learning out of school is an indicator of the interest that now surrounds the role of 'shadow education', which operates alongside the state education system in many countries. To distinguish structured support for school subjects from tutoring for other purposes, Stevenson and Baker (1992) adopted the term 'shadow education', which has since become widely used, as it captures a sense of the private market as one that is shaped by the state education system in a given country and mirrors the school curriculum. As new curricula and forms of assessment are introduced to an education system, the shadow system adapts and grows accordingly. The term 'private supplementary tutoring' is also used to delineate tutoring that supplements lessons in schools and is provided for financial gain (Bray and Kwok, 2003).

Historically, private tutoring dates back over 2,000 years, long before schools were established. A reference to private tutoring is made in the historical records of the work of the great philosopher and educator, Aristotle. According to early sources, in 343 or 342 BCE Alexander's father, Philip of Macedon, who held Aristotle in high regard, chose him to be his son's tutor. The image below depicts Alexander (who later became Alexander the Great) with Aristotle in what appears to be a relaxed, one-to-one tutorial. Among other subjects, Aristotle is credited with teaching science and medicine, which Alexander later used when treating soldiers on the battlefield.

At that time in Greece, and in Britain before schools were established, education was reserved for a privileged few, who were expected to be the country's future leaders. In this context, tutors were expected to cover a wide range of subjects; it was also important for them to be of good character, as their role included responsibility for developing their charge's mind and personal qualities.

Now that almost all children are educated in schools, the role of the tutor has changed in several important ways. Most obviously, schoolteachers are responsible for teaching the national curriculum and generally the task of a tutor is to supplement work covered in the classroom. As a consequence, tutors have become more specialised and they usually offer tuition in only a small number of subjects. Nevertheless, in most countries private tutoring remains the preserve of a privileged minority.

Modes of private tutoring

In the past, tutoring was commonly taken to mean 'one-to-one instruction', a definition given by Ellson (1976: 130). This definition has expanded considerably and 'private tutoring' is used to refer to a wide variety of forms that are found around the world (Bray, 2006; Bray and Kwok, 2003). In addition to individual tutoring, private tutors may work with small groups of students in educational centres and franchises, and in some countries, private agencies run after-school centres such as 'juku' in Japan and 'frontistiria' in Greece, where students may be taught in large classes or even lecture halls, with video transmission to audiences in additional rooms.

Private tutoring is also offered over the phone and via the internet so tutors and students may be in different parts of the country, or even in different countries. Several reports have appeared in the press about companies based in India that offer mathematics tutoring. Some of these are large businesses: according to a BBC report (Berg, 2011), the publishing company Pearson announced in January 2011 that it had bought a majority stake in Tutorvista, an Indian online tutoring company, for just under £80m.

In England there is a tradition of one-to-one tuition, which remains the most popular arrangement and may be used for a wide range of subjects. This lecture focuses on one-to-one tuition in the state and private sectors in England, mapping current provision, its effectiveness and quality. It highlights policy options and argues that, for parents, employing private tutors may be an extension of their role and involvement in their children's education.

How extensive is shadow education in England?

Globally, there is wide variation in the extent of shadow education. International surveys suggest that it is less widespread in the UK and several western European countries than in other parts of the world. The 2006 PISA survey included several questions on out-of-school learning and found that just 17 per cent of 15 year olds in England had one-to-one lessons with a teacher outside school, just below the Organisation for Economic Co-operation and Development (OECD) average of 18 per cent (Tunisia topped the table, with over 70 per cent of students receiving tutoring in mathematics). In addition, 7 per cent reported having lessons in a small group and 7 per cent in a larger group of more than 8 students, compared with OECD averages of 11 per cent and 8 per cent respectively (OECD, 2011).

It is useful for stakeholders to know whether the shadow system is expanding, and since the turn of the century four surveys on private tutoring have been undertaken in England. The first, in 2003–4, surveyed over 3,000 students in state-maintained schools in England and found that 8 per cent of students in Year 6 (aged 10 to 11) had a tutor for mathematics, 8 per cent for English and 3 per cent for science. Similarly, among students in Year 11 (aged 15 to 16), 8 per cent had tutoring for maths and 3 per cent for science, with fewer being tutored in English (3 per cent) (Ireson and Rushforth, 2011). Students received similar amounts of private tutoring in any school subject during Years 6, 11 and 13; and more than one in four students (27 per cent) had had a tutor at some point in their educational careers (Ireson and Rushforth, 2005), a figure that was widely reported in the press and broadcast media. This survey used a stratified sampling frame to ensure that there was adequate representation of schools in disadvantaged areas.

A random telephone survey of parents in England during 2008 estimated that 12 per cent of primary school pupils and 8 per cent of secondary school pupils had been tutored in an academic subject (Peters *et al.*, 2009). Estimates of private tuition in Key Stage 2 were 9 per cent in maths/numeracy and 8 per cent in English/literacy, compared to 7 per cent and 4 per cent respectively in Key Stage 4. Children in Years 5 and 6 were most likely to receive private tuition, with rates of 13 per cent in maths/numeracy and 11 per cent in English/literacy. These figures are consistent with those of Ireson and Rushforth (2005, 2011) in showing that there is a high demand for private tutors in the final years of primary school and in mathematics. These figures also suggest that there may have been an increase in tuition for Year 6 pupils since the earlier 2003–4 survey.

Given the different questions and samples in the surveys mentioned above, there is some uncertainty about the extent of any increase in private tuition. Two surveys undertaken for the Sutton Trust (Ipsos MORI, 2005, 2009) are valuable in this respect, as they included similar questions on private tutoring in nationally representative samples of pupils aged 11 to 16 in over 100 secondary and middle schools. In 2009 one in five pupils (22 per cent) said they received private or home tuition, an increase of four percentage points since 2005 (18 per cent). There was also a large increase in the proportion of pupils in London who received private tutoring, from 36 per cent in 2005 to 43 per cent in 2009. Young people in London were significantly more likely than average to receive private or home tutoring (43 per cent compared with 22 per cent overall).

Parents who live in areas where there is competition for places in selective secondary schools appear more likely to employ tutors for their children during the final years of primary school. A recent survey in two grammar schools, one for girls and one for boys, found that 72 per cent of the students reported having had private tuition in school subjects or for a school entrance examination prior to entry, when they were still in primary school. This survey was undertaken when students were in Year 7, shortly after they started grammar school, and shows that 67 per cent of boys and girls had a private tutor; a further 3 per cent of boys and 8 per cent of girls received extra tuition in a class or group, with 4 per cent receiving both types of tuition (Brown and Ireson, in preparation).

It is worth noting that the students in all these surveys were attending state-maintained schools, so it is not possible to draw any direct comparisons with the independent, fee-paying sector. Research in the Republic of Ireland suggests that private tuition may be widespread in the independent sector: it shows a higher rate of participation in private tuition among students attending fee-paying schools than among those attending other types of school (Smyth, 2009: 10). According to the 2006 PISA survey, similar proportions of students in UK public and private schools participate in out-of-school lessons with someone who is not their schoolteacher. This suggests that the shadow system is shaped not only by the state education system but also by the independent sector.

Who provides tutoring?

Parents told us that they found private tutors mainly through word of mouth recommendations, just as you might find a plumber or electrician (Ireson and Rushforth, 2005). In 2008 the government commissioned the National Centre for Social Research (NatCen) and the Institute of Education, University of London (IOE) to investigate the market of private tuition providers for students in Key Stages 1–4 in England. Realising that it would not be feasible to provide a complete map of provision as so many tutors do not advertise their services, we based our research on information available on the internet. Web searches identified 504 private tuition agencies in England, the majority of which operated regionally (86 per cent), with a small number operating nationally (14 per cent). Regional agencies tended to be concentrated in London (32 per cent) and the South East (25 per cent), and in cities such as Manchester and

Birmingham. Most agencies offered tutoring in maths (97 per cent) and English (93 per cent), followed by science (78 per cent) and languages (61 per cent). Tuition in other subjects was offered, but by less than half of the participating agencies. Most tuition was offered on a one-to-one basis (78 per cent), with group tuition mentioned as the main mode by one in five of the agencies in the survey (Tanner *et al.*, 2009).

Agencies that advertised their services on the internet differed somewhat in their business practice. Some operated in a traditional way, whereas others used their web pages rather like a notice board.

Traditional agencies: maintain a list of registered tutors and allocate work in response to requests from prospective clients.

Notice board: agency maintains a website notice board for individual tutor advertisements with contact details, allowing clients to negotiate directly with the tutors.

Mediated notice board: agency maintains a list of registered tutors from which clients select, but no individual tutor contact details are provided, so the contract with the tutor occurs solely through the agency.

Individual/small agencies: consist of individual tutors or informal professional networks of tutors that allow work to be shared out or passed along.

Educational centre: tuition takes place at a designated location, often solely dedicated to providing tuition. Some of these are franchise operations.

Looking at tutor qualifications, 43 per cent of agencies in the survey reported that all their tutors had a teaching qualification or Qualified Teacher Status (QTS) and 22 per cent had a degree in the subject taught. Two-thirds of small agencies reported that all their tutors had teaching qualifications, compared to 16 per cent of large agencies. These figures mean that although most agency tutors are qualified to teach, or have a university degree, a sizeable number of tutors have neither of these qualifications. The onus is on the parent to check the tutor's background, particularly when locating a tutor from a website notice board.

The majority of agencies (79 per cent) carried out Criminal Records Bureau (CRB) checks on all their tutors. While this figure is relatively high, it means that about one in five agencies does not require its tutors to have CRB checks. Some tutors offered parents and students reassurances of personal safety through the arrangements they made for tutorials. These included leaving the door open or inviting parents to sit in on a tutorial. Some tutors would only provide tuition in the student's home.

Costs of private tuition

For families that employ private tutors, the costs can be significant, with agencies reporting fees of £24 on average (median) for a one-hour tutorial in 2008. Fees in London and the South East tend to be higher than those in the North of England (Tanner *et al.*, 2009) and rise slightly with Key Stage level. Given that tutoring often extends for two terms or more, the cost per subject could be around £600. However, costs vary widely, from £10 to £60 per session, with a small number of agencies reporting typical costs of £10 per hour, which may suggest a 'Robin Hood' effect of discounting for parents in difficult economic circumstances. Various additional fees are charged for specialised diagnostic assessments, travel costs and so on.

Unsurprisingly, in view of the costs involved, the take-up of private tuition is linked to parental education and occupation. Several studies in England and Ireland show that parents in managerial and professional occupations are more likely to employ tutors than parents who are semi-skilled or unskilled (Ireson and Rushforth, 2011; Peters *et al.*, 2009; Smyth, 2009). Ireson and Rushforth (2011) found that parents who had degree level qualifications were more likely than those with college or school education to employ tutors, especially for children in Year 11.

One-to-one tuition in schools

A certain amount of one-to-one tuition is provided in schools, mainly for children who make slow progress in literacy and numeracy. Recent initiatives include 'Every Child a Reader' (ECaR) (Every Child a Chance Trust, 2009a) and 'Every Child Counts' (Every Child a Chance Trust, 2009b) which aim to enable specific groups of children with low attainment to make progress in primary school.

'Reading Recovery', originally developed in New Zealand and subsequently based at the IOE, formed a foundation for the ECaR initiative. Reading Recovery is a well-established and researched programme which targets children, aged five or six, who are the lowest literacy achievers after their first year of school (http://readingrecovery.ioe.ac.uk/). As part of the ECaR initiative, Reading Recovery teachers offer more phonics instruction, alongside other literacy programmes, and also support other teachers in the school. Similarly, the 'Numbers Count' programme, developed at Edge Hill University in England and launched in September 2008, aims to enable Year 2 children who have the greatest difficulty to make progress in numeracy and achieve expected targets for their age. Both programmes provide one-to-one tuition by trained teachers who deploy a specific set of activities and resources. The government has committed to funding ECaR through the Dedicated Schools Grant, until the summer of 2014, though it will be up to schools to decide whether to use the funds for this purpose.

In addition to these initiatives, the former Labour government introduced a scheme to provide one-to-one tuition in primary and secondary schools. England was one of several countries, alongside the USA and Australia, to adopt one-to-one tuition as a supplement to publicly funded school education. In the USA, legislation introduced under the 'No Child Left Behind' Act of 2001 required that eligible students must be provided with private tutoring in reading and mathematics out of school hours (Burch and Good, 2009). In Australia, the federal government introduced 'An Even Start', which gave parents a choice of school-based tuition or private tuition (Watson, 2009). In England, the Making Good Progress (MGP) scheme, launched in 2007, included one-to-one tuition in English and mathematics as one of several elements that aimed to improve achievement for pupils aged 7 to 14 (Key Stages 2 and 3). In the project schools, pupils who fell behind others in their class were offered ten hours of one-to-one tuition. As with ECaR, funding for one-to-one tuition is included in school budgets through the Dedicated Schools Grant until summer 2014 and will not be ring-fenced, so schools are not obliged to use it for that purpose.

Does one-to-one tuition raise attainment?

Given the costs of one-to-one tuition, whether provided in the state or shadow system, a crucial issue is whether it is effective in raising attainment. This turns out to be a complex issue due to differences in the characteristics of tutors and their tutees, the subject matter covered and the lack of well-established quality indicators. Several reviews of the literature conclude that the effects of one-to-one tuition in school subjects are variable. Some studies find positive effects (e.g. Bunting and Mooney, 2001; Mischo and Haag, 2002), some show mixed effects (Ireson and Rushforth, 2005; Rushforth, 2011) and some show no effects (Smyth, 2008, 2009). When school-based tutoring programmes in literacy are compared, some achieve much better results than others (Elbaum *et al.*, 2000).

Our evaluation of private tutoring in England found limited effects on achievement in English, whereas tutoring in maths appeared to have an impact on GCSE grades (Ireson, 2005; Ireson and Rushforth, 2005; Rushforth, 2011). An initial analysis of data collected from 296 Year 11 students who took their GCSEs in 2003 found that tutoring in mathematics raised pupil achievement by about half a GCSE grade, whereas tutoring in English had a negligible impact on English grades (Ireson, 2005; Ireson and Rushforth, 2005). This analysis controlled statistically for students' prior attainment, gender, eligibility for free school meals, ethnicity and family background. It was later extended by Rushforth (2011) who included a larger sample and confirmed the impact of private tutoring on attainment in mathematics; it also found that students who had longer periods of tuition, amounting to two or more terms during Key Stage 4, achieved 0.4 of a GCSE grade higher, on average, than students who had no mathematics tuition during Years 10 and 11.

Smyth (2008, 2009) reported no positive effects of private tutoring on Irish students' performance at the end of the secondary phase of their education. These analyses also controlled for differences between students who did and did not participate in tuition and found that even relatively high levels of private tuition did not enhance students' performance.

Turning to one-to-one tuition in schools, the Making Good Progress Pilot included ten hours of 'Progression tuition' for pupils in Key Stages 2 and 3 (aged 7 to 14 years) who were below the expected national curriculum level or making slow progress. An evaluation of the one-to-one tuition used teacher assessment data to calculate the number of sub-levels gained by each pupil (PricewaterhouseCoopers LLP, 2010). The findings suggested that one-to-one tuition had a positive effect on children's reading but there was no significant impact on writing or mathematics. This analysis compared children who received tuition with those who did not and also controlled statistically for pupil characteristics that are known to influence attainment. Additional analysis suggested that pupils with low prior attainment who received tuition were more likely to achieve level 4 at Key Stage 2 in reading, writing and mathematics and to make two levels of progress. Progress was greater in the first two years of the project, but the authors note that in the early stages of the project, when new processes and practices were being embedded, the reliability of teacher assessment data was low, and for this reason the findings should be treated with extreme caution.

Reading Recovery, which has been subject to several evaluative studies, has shown to be successful in raising the reading levels of children who complete the programme (e.g. Hurry and Sylva, 2007; Pinnell *et al.*, 1994). However, it is not suitable for all children and the programme is discontinued for those who do not make satisfactory progress. During 2008–9 in ECaR schools, children receiving one-to-one literacy tuition gained 21 months in reading age, on average, over the year. Over three-quarters of children (78 per cent) reached average levels of literacy for their age after approximately 40 hours of daily one-to-one teaching. Similar children in comparison schools made seven months' progress over the year (Every Child a Chance Trust, 2009a).

Numbers Count succeeded in raising children's 'number age' by 13.5 months in an average of 2.9 calendar months of one-to-one tuition. Children were almost a year (10.6 months) behind their calendar ages when they started the programme (Every Child a Chance Trust, 2009b). An independent evaluation reported a statistically significant difference in mathematics test scores for children who received Numbers Count tuition when compared with an equivalent group of children who did not (Torgerson *et al.*, 2011). The standard mathematics test (Progress in Maths 6/7) was independently administered and findings show an effect size of 0.33, which is equivalent to 7 additional weeks' improvement for children who received Numbers Count compared with children who did not. Teaching in pairs was found to be as effective as one-to-one tuition.

Evidently, one-to-one tuition is not 'a panacea', as Shanahan pointed out with reference to the teaching of reading (1998: 221). It can be very effective, but its impact depends on the content of tutoring sessions and the quality of tutoring. The success of carefully designed literacy and numeracy programmes for specific target groups shows that it is possible to raise attainment for the majority of low attaining children in the early years of primary school.

Studies of the effectiveness of private tutoring show that it can be effective, but results are not guaranteed. Researchers have rarely included indicators of quality, which thus remain an uncontrolled variable in much research and may go some way to explaining inconsistencies in findings. There is still a great deal to learn about the general components of effective tutoring and the elements required for different subject matter and students.

It is also worth noting that short bursts of tutoring may not be effective in the longer term. For example, Hurry and Sylva (2007) questioned the long-term effects of Reading Recovery and suggest that additional intervention may be needed at a later stage. Results of Numbers Count indicate that children continued to make progress after the end of the programme (Every Child a Chance Trust, 2009b), though a longer term follow-up is needed to check whether this progress is maintained. Students may benefit from individual support at more than one point in their learning.

What makes one-to-one tuition special?

In our survey of students and parents, we found that the main reasons for having a tutor were to do well in tests and examinations, to increase understanding and to develop confidence (Ireson and Rushforth, 2011). By implication, tutors must be prepared to help students with both the cognitive and affective aspects of learning. Thanks to a growing body of research we now have a much better understanding of the cognitive aspects and are beginning to uncover components of the motivational and emotional side of one-to-one tuition.

Clearly, the main advantage of one-to-one tuition is that work can be tailored to the student's needs. Although this is easier to achieve in a one-to-one setting than in a busy classroom, even trained teachers can find individual tutoring difficult (Bennett *et al.*, 1984; Lesh and Kelly, 1997), particularly with students who have special educational needs (Ireson and Evans, 1995). A one-to-one tutorial places extra demands on both tutors and students as it is 'more individualised, immediate and interactive than most school settings' (Lepper and Woolverton, 2002: 138). To effectively tailor work to a student's needs calls for knowledge of the subject matter, a model of the student's current knowledge as well as pedagogical knowledge, or how to teach the current topic (Lepper and Woolverton, 2002; McArthur *et al.*, 1990; Merrill *et al.*, 1992; Wood and Wood, 1996).

Skilful tutors are sensitive to their student's cognitive state and they employ a variety of strategies to ensure that tasks presented are sufficiently challenging, yet not too demanding (Merrill *et al.*, 1992; McArthur *et al.*, 1990). This is achieved through structuring and adjusting a learning activity before and during the tutorial. When selecting the next learning activity, a tutor builds on what the learner already knows and can do, and also bears in mind the student's preferences for approaching a topic and his or her interest in different types of activity.

Photo: Philip Meech

During a tutorial, tutors continue the process of task structuring by adjusting the support they provide while the student is working on a task. More direct forms of guidance, such as demonstrating a task, may be used if the student is having difficulty or if the material is new, whereas hints and prompts may be sufficient if the learning activity is less challenging (Wood and Wood, 1996). A skilled tutor flexibly adjusts support during the tutorial, with the aim of enabling the student to reach a learning goal with a minimum of assistance. Flexible tutors also recognise that learners take different paths and are prepared to follow and support them along the way.

Teacher feedback is one of the most powerful factors affecting learning (Hattie, 2002; Wiliam, 2009) and expert teachers monitor their students' progress and provide relevant, useful feedback. In general, skilled tutors provide positive feedback for correct answers; however, they tend to respond indirectly to student errors that they judge to be unimportant rather than correcting them immediately (Graesser and Person, 1994). Instead, they use information from student errors to help adjust the amount of support they offer. As mathematics teachers become more experienced and proficient in tutoring, they tend to become less directive and use implicit guidance strategies that follow students' thinking as opposed to asking closed questions and funnelling students' thinking towards correct answers (Lesh and Kelly, 1997). The use of open questions encourages students' thinking and self-regulation.

Tutors believe that for successful tutoring, it is critical that the student is fully committed to the tuition and ready to take an active part in their learning (Tanner *et al.*, 2009: 69). Students value the chance to ask any questions in the tutorial environment as this is not always possible in a busy classroom (Ireson and Rushforth, 2011). Students' questions are also valuable for the tutor, as they help to identify the starting point for learning and help to identify areas of misunderstanding. For some students this exposure can be threatening and requires a good level of trust in the tutor.

Tutors seek to gain students' trust in them as a tutor by being friendly, personable and patient (Tanner *et al.*, 2009: 69). Both tutors and students agree that establishing and maintaining rapport is an element of effective tutoring practice, along with the ability to provide clear explanations, patience and good communication skills (Rushforth, 2011). Students gain trust if they perceive the tutor to be genuinely interested in their learning and capable of helping them to learn.

Lepper and Woolverton (2002) propose that tutors maintain two independent models of the student's cognitive and affective state and may encounter situations where the implications of the two models conflict. For example, the tutor may feel that the student does not fully understand the work, but the student may be very keen to move on. In this situation the tutor may find a way of presenting a problem that makes it look more difficult, or move on to a more difficult problem and provide a high level of scaffolding support. Conflict situations can be challenging for a tutor.

Parental involvement

As this brief sketch of effective tutoring shows, one-to-one tuition can be challenging, yet paradoxically, parents and other family members can and do provide a level of support for their children's learning at home (Ireson and Rushforth, submitted). Parents feel more capable of helping their children with the primary school curriculum than with GCSE or A- level work, with almost two-thirds of Year 6 parents (64 per cent) indicating that they did not need to employ a tutor as the family provided enough help (Ireson and Rushforth, 2011). Given that the employment of tutors was just as high in Year 6 as in Year 11, this suggests that much of the Year 6 demand is from parents who employ tutors to prepare children for the 11 Plus, Common Entrance, Key Stage 2 tests and other examinations used in the secondary school selection process.

During interviews, parents referred to specific levels of achievement required by their child to progress to the next phase of education. In an area where the 11 Plus examination was used to select pupils for entry to grammar schools, parents were conscious of the need for their child to do well and were often aware that other parents employed tutors. Comments such as 'a lot of them had tutors to get them through the 11 Plus' were made by several parents. Similarly, a realisation that their child was unlikely to achieve the specific GCSE grades required for entry to a desired college course or to be allowed to progress to Year 13 or achieve the A-level grades required for entry to university also prompted parents to consider employing a tutor. Parents appear to calibrate their child's progress in school against the capacity of the family to help, and many monitor the situation: as one parent put it, 'I feel that I'm enough for her at the moment.' Although this parent felt able to provide sufficient support at present, she was keeping an eye on her child's progress and would employ a tutor if needed (Ireson and Rushforth, submitted).

The frequency of assessment and target setting in schools, coupled with information about the grades needed for desirable schools or courses, all encourage students and their parents to consider whether to seek additional help. Some parents feel unable to support their child's learning in certain subjects or may not be familiar with a specific examination syllabus. Others feel able to support their child but have insufficient time to do so, and some report finding it less stressful to have help from a tutor as this alleviates what might be difficult interactions between themselves and their child if they try to help. Clearly, though, many parents in England see it as part of their parental role to support their children's learning in school and private tutoring may be a substitute, or an extension, of that role.

Conclusion and future directions

Private tutoring is an attractive option for many students and their parents as well as for tutors and agencies of various types. For parents and students, some of the perceived benefits include improved performance in tests and examinations, increased confidence and better understanding of a subject. Tutors also assist with study strategies and may be employed to teach subjects that are not covered in school. Disadvantages for parents include the costs of employment, the difficulty of finding a suitable tutor and the lack of regulation, as anyone can offer their services as a tutor. Parents may not see the results they hope for and *caveat emptor* is just as true in employing a tutor as with purchasing any other service.

Private tutoring can be a fulfilling occupation for tutors who work with willing students and see them make progress. For some it provides an interesting environment where they are free from the perceived constraints and bureaucracy of classroom teaching. Hours are flexible and income is often cash in hand.

From a national perspective, a major concern about shadow education is that it increases social and economic inequalities. More affluent parents tend to use private tutoring to help their children make successful transitions in the education system. Tutoring is very prevalent in areas where there is intense competition for places in popular schools and parents who can afford tutors may be able to secure a competitive advantage for their children, thus closing down the options for students from less wealthy families.

Although at present the size of the shadow system may not be a major concern in England, it is worth looking to other countries where shadow education is much more prevalent and considering its impact. When shadow education becomes extensive, it can have a negative effect on mainstream education as teachers may put less effort into their classroom teaching when they realise that students will cover the work with their tutors. Cases of unethical practice have been uncovered in countries where teachers offer extra tuition to students in their own classes at the end of the normal school day, to cover the examination syllabus (Silova, 2009). Students who cannot afford extra tuition miss out on this crucial preparation for the next phase of education. Impacts on classroom teaching also include teachers paying more attention to students who are not tutored or favouring the students they tutor themselves (Silova, 2009). In Japan, the shadow system has held back some attempts to reform the state education system (Baker and LeTendre, 2005).

To date, the UK government has shown little inclination to develop policy for the shadow market and has not considered any form of registration for tutors, though this approach has been taken elsewhere to provide quality assurance for parents. Instead, the previous government invested in one-to-one tuition programmes in school, which have enabled some of the lowest attaining children to achieve expected standards. An important point about this provision is that, together with after-school clubs, revision classes and booster sessions, it provides opportunities that are accessible to all, including students from less advantaged backgrounds. In future, schools will be expected to take more responsibility for one-to-one tuition, and it remains to be seen whether promising programmes survive.

Acknowledgements

Many people contributed to the research on shadow education in England, including Katie Rushforth, who was the lead researcher for 'Mapping and evaluating shadow education', a project funded by the Economic and Social Research Council (ESRC). I am grateful to the ESRC for funding this work at a time when shadow education was barely on the radar in the UK. Katie contributed to several other projects and went on to complete a PhD on the quality and effectiveness of private tutoring.

Steven Finch and Emily Tanner at NatCen collaborated on a survey of private tuition providers, commissioned by the DCSF. Penelope Brown contributed to several projects, including a survey of students in two grammar schools about private tutoring prior to entry. Paul Bassett provided valuable statistical advice on several projects, and other researchers include Marianna Sanderson and Kelvin Smith.

I am grateful to my family for their continuing support and interest.

Last but not least, special thanks to the many tutors, schools, teachers and students who made arrangements for us, found time to talk about their experiences and completed questionnaires, and without whom this lecture would not have been possible.

References

Baker, D. and LeTendre, G. (2005) *National Differences, Global Similarities: World culture and the future of schooling*. Stanford, CA: Stanford University Press.

Bennett, N., Desforges, C., Coburn, A. and Wilkinson, C. (1984) *The Quality of Pupil Learning Experiences*. London: Lawrence Erlbaum Associates.

Berg, S. 'Pearson moves into online tutoring'. *BBC Today Programme*, 21 January 2011; available at: http://news.bbc.co.uk/today/hi/today/newsid_9369000/9369185.stm

Bray, M. (1999) *The Shadow Education System: Private tutoring and its implications for planners*. Paris: UNESCO and International Institute for Educational Planning (IIEP).

-- (2006) 'Private supplementary tutoring: Comparative perspectives on patterns and implications'. *Compare*, 36(4), 515–30.

-- (forthcoming 2011) 'The challenge of shadow education: Private tutoring and its implications for policy makers in the European Union'. Unpublished draft.

Bray, M. and Kwok, P. (2003) 'Demand for private supplementary tutoring: Conceptual considerations and socio-economic patterns in Hong Kong'. *Economics of Education Review*, 22(6), 611–20.

Brown, P. and Ireson, J. (in preparation) 'Making the grade: Private tutoring for a place in grammar school'.

Bunting, B.P. and Mooney, E. (2001) 'The effects of practice and coaching on test results for educational selection at eleven years of age'. *Educational Psychology*, 21(3), 243–53.

Burch, P. and Good, A. (2009) 'Getting to the core: The role of instructional setting in federally mandated tutoring'. Paper presented to the annual meeting of the American Educational Research Association, San Diego, CA., 13-19 April.

Elbaum, B., Vaughn, S., Hughes, M.T. and Moody, S.W. (2000) 'How effective are one-to-one tutoring programmes in reading for elementary students at risk for reading failure? A meta-analysis of the intervention research'. *Journal of Educational Psychology*, 92(4), 605–19.

Ellson, D.G. (1976) 'Tutoring'. In N.L. Gage (ed.) *The Psychology of Teaching Methods*. Chicago: University of Chicago Press.

European Centre for Reading Recovery (2011) *Every Child A Reader: Annual Report 2009–10*. London: IOE/ECRR.

Every Child a Chance Trust (2009a) *Every Child a Reader: The first year of the national roll-out*. London: Every Child a Chance Trust.

-- (2009b) *Every Child Counts: The results of the first year 2008/09*. London: Every Child a Chance Trust.

Graesser, A.C. and Person, N.K. (1994) 'Question asking during tutoring'. *American Educational Research Journal*, 31(1), 104–37.

Hattie, J.A.C. (2002) 'What are the attributes of excellent teachers?' In *Teachers Make a Difference: What is the research evidence?* Wellington: New Zealand Council for Educational Research, 3–26.

Hurry, J. and Sylva, K. (2007) 'Long-term outcomes of early reading intervention'. *Journal of Research in Reading*, 30(3), 227–48.

Ipsos MORI (2005) *Schools Omnibus 2005 (Wave 11)*. London: The Sutton Trust.

-- (2009) *Young People Omnibus (Wave 15)*. London: The Sutton Trust.

Ireson, J. (2004) 'Private tutoring: How prevalent and effective is it?'. *London Review of Education*, 2(2), 109–22.

-- (2005) 'Evaluating the impact of individual tutoring on GCSE attainment'. Paper presented at the British Educational Research Association Annual Conference, University of Glamorgan, 14–17 September.

Ireson, J. and Evans, P. (1995) 'No easy task: Structuring the curriculum for children experiencing difficulties in school'. In B. Norwich and I. Lunt (eds) *Psychology and Education for Special Needs: Recent developments and future directions*. Aldershot: Arena Ashgate, 87–105.

Ireson, J. and Rushforth, K. (2005) *Mapping and Evaluating Shadow Education. Final Report to the Economic and Social Research Council*. London: Institute of Education, University of London (IOE).

-- (2011) 'Private tutoring in the English education system: Its nature, extent and purpose'. *Research Papers in Education*, 26(1), 1–19. (First published on 6 November 2009 (iFirst)).

-- (submitted) 'Individual and contextual factors that influence children's participation in private tutoring in England'.

Lepper, M.R. and Woolverton, M. (2002) 'The wisdom of practice: Lessons learned from the study of highly effective tutors'. In J.M. Aronson (ed.) *Improving Academic Achievement: Impact of psychological factors on education.* Amsterdam: Academic Press, 135–58.

Lesh, R. and Kelly, A.E. (1997) 'Teachers' evolving conceptions of 1-to-1 tutoring: A 3-tiered teaching experiment'. *Journal for research in mathematics education,* 29(4), 398–430.

McArthur, D., Stasz, C. and Zmuidzinas, M. (1990) 'Tutoring techniques in algebra'. *Cognition and Instruction,* 7, 197–244.

Merrill, D., Reiser, B.J., Ranney, M. and Trafton, J.G. (1992) 'Effective tutoring techniques: A comparison of human tutors and intelligent tutoring systems'. *The Journal of the Learning Sciences,* 2, 277–306.

Mischo, C. and Haag, L. (2002) 'Expansion and effectiveness of private tutoring'. *European Journal of Psychology of Education,* XVII(3), 263–73.

Organisation for Economic Co-operation and Development (OECD) (2011) *Quality Time for Students: Learning in and out of school.* Paris: OECD.

Peters, M., Carpenter, H., Edwards, G. and Coleman, N. (2009) *Private Tuition: Survey of parents and carers.* Research Brief DCSF-RBX-09-01. London: Department for Children, Schools and Families (DCSF).

Pinnell, G.S., Lyons, C.A., DeFord, D.E., Bryck, A. and Selzer, M. (1994) 'Comparing instructional models for the literacy education of high-risk first graders'. *Reading Research Quarterly,* 29, 8–39.

PricewaterhouseCoopers LLP (2010) *Evaluation of the Making Good Progress Pilot.* Research Report DCSF-RR184. London: DCSF.

Rushforth, K. (2011) 'Quality and effectiveness of one-to-one private tuition in England'. Unpublished PhD thesis, IOE.

Shanahan, T. (1998) 'On the effectiveness and limitations of tutoring in reading'. *Review of Research in Education,* 23, 217–34.

Silova, I. (2009) 'Private tutoring in Eastern Europe and Central Asia'. Paper presented to the annual meeting of the American Educational Research Association, San Diego, CA.,13–19 April.

Smyth, E. (2008) 'The more the better? Intensity of involvement in private tuition and examination performance'. *Educational Research and Evaluation*, 14(5), 465–76.

-- (2009) 'Buying your way into college? Private tuition and the transition to higher education in Ireland'. *Oxford Review of Education*, 35 (1), 1–22.

Stevenson, D.L. and Baker, D.P. (1992) 'Shadow education and allocation in formal schooling: Transition to university in Japan'. *American Journal of Sociology*, 97(6), 1639–57.

Tanner, E., Ireson, J., Day, N., Rushforth, K., Tennant, R., Turczuk, O. and Smith, K. (2009) *Private Tuition in England*. Research Report DCSF-RR081. London: DCSF, 1–126.

Torgerson, C.J., Wiggins, A., Torgerson, D.J., Ainsworth, H., Barmby, P., Hewitt, C., Jones, K., Hendry, V., Askew, M., Bland, M., Coe, R., Higgins, S., Hodgen, J., Hulme, C. and Tymms, P. (2011) *Every Child Counts: The independent evaluation – Technical report*. Research Report DFE-RR091A. London: Department for Education.

Watson, L. (2009) 'Public and private expenditure on supplementary tutoring in Australia: The structural, political and economic context of recent developments'. Paper presented to the annual meeting of the American Educational Research Association, San Diego, 13–19 April.

Wiliam, D. (2009) *Assessment for Learning: Why, what and how?* London: IOE.

Wood, D. and Wood, H. (1996) 'Vygotsky, tutoring and learning'. *Oxford Review of Education*, 22(1) 5–16.